OLD IS THE NEW YOUNG

summersdale

OLD IS THE NEW YOUNG

First published in 2011

This edition copyright © Summersdale Publishers Ltd, 2016

Summersdale Publishers Ltd
46 West Street
Chichester
West Sussex
PO19 1RP
UK

www.summersdale.com

Printed and bound in the Czech Republic

ISBN: 978-1-84953-820-6

TO.....*Eileen*.................................

FROM...*Ena*...................................

INSIDE EVERY
OLDER PERSON IS A
YOUNGER PERSON
WONDERING WHAT THE
HELL HAPPENED.

Cora Harvey Armstrong

MY WIFE SAID TO ME,
'I DON'T LOOK FIFTY,
DO I DARLING?' I SAID
'NOT ANY MORE.'

Bob Monkhouse

YOU ONLY LIVE ONCE,
BUT IF YOU DO IT RIGHT,
ONCE IS ENOUGH.

Mae West

DON'T LET AGEING GET
YOU DOWN. IT'S TOO
HARD TO GET BACK UP.

John Wagner

OLD AGE AIN'T NO PLACE FOR SISSIES.

Bette Davis

THREE THINGS HAPPEN
WHEN YOU GET TO
MY AGE. FIRST YOUR
MEMORY STARTS TO
GO... I'VE FORGOTTEN
THE OTHER TWO.

Denis Healey

SEIZE THE MOMENT.
REMEMBER ALL THOSE
WOMEN ON THE *TITANIC*
WHO WAVED OFF THE
DESSERT CART.

Erma Bombeck

I HAVE THE BODY OF AN 18-YEAR-OLD. I KEEP IT IN THE FRIDGE.

Spike Milligan

THE OLDER ONE
GROWS, THE MORE ONE
LIKES INDECENCY.

Virginia Woolf

BEAUTIFUL YOUNG
PEOPLE ARE ACCIDENTS
OF NATURE, BUT
BEAUTIFUL OLD PEOPLE
ARE WORKS OF ART.

Eleanor Roosevelt

I'M NOT SIXTY,
I'M 'SEXTY'.

Dolly Parton

EVENTUALLY YOU WILL
REACH A POINT WHEN
YOU STOP LYING ABOUT
YOUR AGE AND START
BRAGGING ABOUT IT.

Will Rogers

YOU CAN'T TURN BACK
THE CLOCK. BUT YOU
CAN WIND IT UP AGAIN.

Bonnie Prudden

IT'S SEX, NOT YOUTH,
THAT'S WASTED ON
THE YOUNG.

Janet Harris

WE ARE YOUNG ONLY
ONCE; AFTER THAT
WE NEED SOME
OTHER EXCUSE.

Anonymous

MY DOCTOR TOLD ME
TO DO SOMETHING
THAT PUTS ME OUT OF
BREATH, SO I'VE TAKEN
UP SMOKING AGAIN.

Jo Brand

MEN ARE LIKE WINE.
SOME TURN TO
VINEGAR, BUT THE BEST
IMPROVE WITH AGE.

C. E. M. Joad

THE AGEING PROCESS
HAS YOU FIRMLY IN ITS
GRASP IF YOU NEVER
GET THE URGE TO
THROW A SNOWBALL.

Doug Larson

WHEN THEY TELL ME
I'M TOO OLD TO DO
SOMETHING, I ATTEMPT
IT IMMEDIATELY.

Pablo Picasso

THE KEY TO SUCCESSFUL
AGEING IS TO PAY AS
LITTLE ATTENTION
TO IT AS POSSIBLE.

Judith Regan

THE BEST TUNES ARE PLAYED ON THE OLDEST FIDDLES.

Ralph Waldo Emerson

AS FOR ME, EXCEPT FOR
AN OCCASIONAL HEART
ATTACK, I FEEL AS
YOUNG AS I EVER DID.

Robert Benchley

OLD AGE IS AN
EXCELLENT TIME FOR
OUTRAGE. MY GOAL
IS TO DO AT LEAST
ONE OUTRAGEOUS
THING EVERY WEEK.

Maggie Kuhn

I DON'T WANT TO RETIRE.
I'M NOT THAT GOOD AT
CROSSWORD PUZZLES.

Norman Mailer

I'M AIMING BY THE TIME I'M 50 TO STOP BEING AN ADOLESCENT.

Wendy Cope

MEN CHASE GOLF
BALLS WHEN THEY'RE
TOO OLD TO CHASE
ANYTHING ELSE.

Groucho Marx

FIRST, YOU FORGET
NAMES... NEXT, YOU
FORGET TO PULL
YOUR ZIPPER UP AND
FINALLY YOU FORGET
TO PULL IT DOWN.

Leo Rosenberg

YOU CAN'T HELP
GETTING OLDER,
BUT YOU DON'T
HAVE TO GET OLD.

George Burns

I'D HATE TO DIE WITH A
GOOD LIVER... WHEN I
DIE I WANT EVERYTHING
TO BE KNACKERED.

Hamish Imlach

I'M OFFICIALLY
MIDDLE-AGED. I DON'T
NEED DRUGS... I CAN
GET THE SAME EFFECT
JUST BY STANDING
UP REAL FAST.

Jonathan Katz

I'M LIMITLESS AS FAR
AS AGE IS CONCERNED...
AS LONG AS HE HAS A
DRIVER'S LICENCE.

Kim Cattrall
on dating younger men

TO GET BACK MY YOUTH
I WOULD DO ANYTHING
IN THE WORLD, EXCEPT
TAKE EXERCISE,
GET UP EARLY, OR
BE RESPECTABLE.

Oscar Wilde

YOU KNOW YOU ARE GETTING OLDER WHEN 'HAPPY HOUR' IS A NAP.

Gary Kristofferson

BE KIND TO YOUR KIDS;
THEY'LL BE CHOOSING
YOUR NURSING HOME.

Anonymous

THERE IS ONLY ONE
CURE FOR GREY HAIR.
IT WAS INVENTED BY
A FRENCHMAN. IT IS
CALLED THE GUILLOTINE.

P. G. Wodehouse

AGE IS JUST A
NUMBER. IT'S TOTALLY
IRRELEVANT UNLESS, OF
COURSE, YOU HAPPEN TO
BE A BOTTLE OF WINE.

Joan Collins

I WANT TO LIVE TO
BE 80 SO I CAN PISS
MORE PEOPLE OFF.

Charles Bukowski

WHEN PEOPLE ARE
OLD ENOUGH TO KNOW
BETTER, THEY'RE OLD
ENOUGH TO DO WORSE.

Hesketh Pearson

PASSING THE VODKA BOTTLE AND PLAYING THE GUITAR.

Keith Richards on how he keeps fit

FEW WOMEN ADMIT
THEIR AGE. FEW
MEN ACT THEIRS.

Anonymous

IF YOU OBEY ALL THE
RULES, YOU MISS
ALL THE FUN.

Katharine Hepburn

I'LL KEEP SWIVELLING
MY HIPS UNTIL THEY
NEED REPLACING.

Tom Jones

I CAN STILL REMEMBER
WHEN THE AIR WAS
CLEAN AND THE
SEX WAS DIRTY.

George Burns

MY GRANDMOTHER'S
90. SHE'S DATING.
HE'S 93. THEY NEVER
ARGUE. THEY CAN'T
HEAR EACH OTHER.

Cathy Ladman

THE OLDER I GET, THE OLDER OLD IS.

Tom Baker

A MAN IS ONLY AS OLD AS THE WOMAN HE FEELS.

Groucho Marx

I DON'T PLAN TO GROW
OLD GRACEFULLY. I PLAN
TO HAVE FACELIFTS
UNTIL MY EARS MEET.

Rita Rudner

SEX IN THE SIXTIES IS
GREAT, BUT IMPROVES
IF YOU PULL OVER TO
THE SIDE OF THE ROAD.

Johnny Carson

WE DO NOT STOP PLAYING
BECAUSE WE GROW OLD.
WE GROW OLD BECAUSE
WE STOP PLAYING.

Anonymous

FORTY IS THE OLD AGE
OF YOUTH; FIFTY THE
YOUTH OF OLD AGE.

Victor Hugo

THE ONLY FORM OF EXERCISE I TAKE IS MASSAGE.

Truman Capote

TIME AND TROUBLE WILL
TAME AN ADVANCED
YOUNG WOMAN, BUT AN
ADVANCED OLD WOMAN
IS UNCONTROLLABLE BY
ANY EARTHLY FORCE.

Dorothy L. Sayers

NOT A SHRED OF
EVIDENCE EXISTS IN
FAVOUR OF THE IDEA
THAT LIFE IS SERIOUS.

Brendan Gill

I CAN STILL ENJOY SEX
AT 74. I LIVE AT 75,
SO IT'S NO DISTANCE.

Bob Monkhouse

I'M TOO OLD TO DO THINGS BY HALF.

Lou Reed

AS THE TALK TURNS
TO OLD AGE, I SAY I
AM 49 PLUS VAT.

Lionel Blair

LAUGHTER DOESN'T REQUIRE TEETH.

Bill Newton

DO NOT WORRY ABOUT
AVOIDING TEMPTATION.
AS YOU GROW OLDER
IT WILL AVOID YOU.

Joey Adams

YOU CAN GET AWAY
WITH MURDER WHEN
YOU'RE 71 YEARS OLD.
PEOPLE JUST THINK
I'M A SILLY OLD FOOL.

Bernard Manning

IS IT NOT STRANGE
THAT DESIRE SHOULD SO
MANY YEARS OUTLIVE
PERFORMANCE?

William Shakespeare

I CAN STILL CUT THE
MUSTARD... I JUST NEED
HELP OPENING THE JAR!

Anonymous

OH, TO BE 70 AGAIN.

Georges Clemenceau on seeing a
pretty girl on his 80th birthday

DOCTORS ARE ALWAYS
TELLING US THAT
DRINKING SHORTENS
YOUR LIFE. WELL
I'VE SEEN MORE OLD
DRUNKARDS THAN
OLD DOCTORS.

Edward Phillips

IF I HAD MY LIFE TO
LIVE OVER AGAIN,
I'D MAKE THE SAME
MISTAKES, ONLY SOONER.

Tallulah Bankhead

IF YOU WANT A THING
DONE WELL, GET
A COUPLE OF OLD
BROADS TO DO IT.

Bette Davis

INTERVIEWER: TO WHAT DO YOU ATTRIBUTE YOUR ADVANCED AGE?

MALCOLM SARGENT: WELL, I SUPPOSE I MUST ATTRIBUTE IT TO THE FACT THAT I HAVE NOT DIED.

OLD AGE IS LIKE A
PLANE FLYING THROUGH
A STORM. ONCE YOU
ARE ABOARD THERE IS
NOTHING YOU CAN DO.

Golda Meir

NO MAN IS EVER OLD ENOUGH TO KNOW BETTER.

Holbrook Jackson

ONE OF THE BEST PARTS
OF GROWING OLDER?
YOU CAN FLIRT ALL
YOU LIKE SINCE YOU'VE
BECOME HARMLESS.

Liz Smith

ANOTHER BELIEF OF MINE: THAT EVERYONE ELSE MY AGE IS AN ADULT, WHEREAS I AM MERELY IN DISGUISE.

Margaret Atwood

MY GRANDMOTHER IS
OVER 80 AND STILL
DOESN'T NEED GLASSES.
DRINKS RIGHT OUT
OF THE BOTTLE.

Henny Youngman

ONE SHOULD NEVER
MAKE ONE'S DEBUT
IN A SCANDAL. ONE
SHOULD RESERVE THAT
TO GIVE INTEREST
TO ONE'S OLD AGE.

Oscar Wilde

WHEN I WAS YOUNG,
I WAS TOLD: 'YOU'LL
SEE WHEN YOU'RE 50.'
I'M 50 AND I HAVEN'T
SEEN A THING.

Erik Satie

LIFE IS TOO SHORT TO LEARN GERMAN.

Richard Porson

EXERCISE DAILY.
EAT WISELY.
DIE ANYWAY.

Anonymous

OLD PEOPLE SHOULD
NOT EAT HEALTH
FOODS. THEY NEED ALL
THE PRESERVATIVES
THEY CAN GET.

Robert Orben

INTERVIEWER: CAN YOU REMEMBER ANY OF YOUR PAST LIVES?

THE DALAI LAMA: AT MY AGE I HAVE A PROBLEM REMEMBERING WHAT HAPPENED YESTERDAY.

MIDDLE AGE IS WHEN IT
TAKES YOU ALL NIGHT TO
DO ONCE WHAT ONCE YOU
USED TO DO ALL NIGHT.

Kenny Everett

GROWING OLD IS COMPULSORY, GROWING UP IS OPTIONAL.

Bob Monkhouse

MY GRANDMOTHER
WAS A VERY TOUGH
WOMAN. SHE BURIED
THREE HUSBANDS AND
TWO OF THEM WERE
JUST NAPPING.

Rita Rudner

AS ONE GROWS OLDER,
ONE BECOMES WISER
AND MORE FOOLISH.

François de La Rochefoucauld

THERE IS NO PLEASURE
WORTH FORGOING
JUST FOR AN EXTRA
THREE YEARS IN THE
GERIATRIC WARD.

John Mortimer

I SMOKE 10 TO 15
CIGARS A DAY; AT MY
AGE I HAVE TO HOLD
ON TO SOMETHING.

George Burns

WHEN WE'RE YOUNG
WE WANT TO CHANGE
THE WORLD. WHEN
WE'RE OLD WE WANT TO
CHANGE THE YOUNG.

Anonymous

EVERY MORNING, LIKE
CLOCKWORK, AT 7 A.M., I
PEE. UNFORTUNATELY, I
DON'T WAKE UP TILL 8.

Harry Beckworth

I'M 78 BUT I STILL
USE A CONDOM WHEN
I HAVE SEX. I CAN'T
TAKE THE DAMP.

Alan Gregory

LONG AFTER WEARING
BIFOCALS AND HEARING
AIDS, WE'LL STILL
BE MAKING LOVE.
WE JUST WON'T
KNOW WITH WHOM.

Jack Paar

MY NAN SAID, 'WHAT DO YOU MEAN WHEN YOU SAY THE COMPUTER WENT DOWN ON YOU?'

Joseph Longthorne

AN OLD MAN MARRYING
A YOUNG GIRL IS LIKE
BUYING A BOOK FOR
SOMEONE ELSE TO READ.

Jim Thompson

I WOULDN'T LIKE TO DIE
ON STAGE. I'D SETTLE
FOR ROOM SERVICE
AND A COUPLE OF
DISSIPATED WOMEN.

Peter O'Toole

WHEN I DIE I WANT
TO GO LIKE MY
GRANDFATHER,
PEACEFULLY IN HIS
SLEEP. NOT SCREAMING,
LIKE HIS PASSENGERS.

Anonymous

THE OLDER WE GET, THE BETTER WE USED TO BE.

John McEnroe

BILL WYMAN COULDN'T
BE HERE TONIGHT.
HE'S AT THE HOSPITAL
ATTENDING THE BIRTH
OF HIS NEXT WIFE.

Frank Worthington

IT'S A SOBERING
THOUGHT: WHEN
MOZART WAS MY AGE,
HE HAD BEEN DEAD
FOR TWO YEARS.

Tom Lehrer

THE WIDOWER MARRIED
HIS FIRST WIFE'S
SISTER SO HE WOULDN'T
HAVE TO BREAK IN A
NEW MOTHER-IN-LAW.

Tony Hancock

HERE'S GOD'S CRUEL
JOKE: BY THE TIME
A GUY FIGURES OUT
HOW WOMEN WORK,
HIS PENIS DOESN'T.

Adam Carolla

OLD? HE CHASES HIS
SECRETARY AROUND
THE DESK BUT CAN'T
REMEMBER WHY.

Leopold Fechtner

I'M IN PRETTY GOOD SHAPE FOR THE SHAPE I'M IN.

Mickey Rooney at 58

MIDDLE AGE IS WHEN
YOUR AGE STARTS
TO SHOW AROUND
YOUR MIDDLE.

Bob Hope

DRINKING REMOVES
WARTS AND WRINKLES
FROM WOMEN I LOOK AT.

Jackie Gleason

WHEN I DIE I WANT
TO BE CREMATED, AND
TEN PER CENT OF MY
ASHES THROWN IN
MY AGENT'S FACE.

W. C. Fields

WHY HAVE I LIVED SO
LONG? JACK DANIELS
AND NOT TAKING SHIT
FROM THE PRESS.

Frank Sinatra

MY ONLY REGRET IN LIFE IS THAT I DIDN'T DRINK MORE CHAMPAGNE.

John Maynard Keynes

I HOPE YOU DIE BEFORE
ME BECAUSE I DON'T
WANT YOU SINGING
AT MY FUNERAL.

Spike Milligan to Harry Secombe

EARLY TO RISE AND
EARLY TO BED MAKES
A MAN HEALTHY,
WEALTHY AND DEAD.

James Thurber

DO I EXERCISE? WELL
I ONCE JOGGED TO
THE ASHTRAY.

Will Self

I THINK ALL OLD
FOLKS' HOMES SHOULD
HAVE STRIPTEASE.
IF I RAN ONE I'D
HAVE A STRIPTEASE
EVERY WEEK.

Cynthia Payne

ARE THERE SEXY DEAD ONES?

Sean Connery after being informed he was voted 'The Sexiest Man Alive' in a poll

I HAVEN'T HAD A HIT
FILM SINCE JOAN
COLLINS WAS A VIRGIN.

Burt Reynolds

YOUTH IS WHEN
YOU'RE ALLOWED TO
STAY UP LATE ON
NEW YEAR'S EVE.
MIDDLE AGE IS WHEN
YOU'RE FORCED TO.

Bill Vaughn

THEY SAY YOU
SHOULDN'T SAY
NOTHING ABOUT THE
DEAD UNLESS IT'S GOOD.
HE'S DEAD. GOOD.

Jackie Mabley

ALWAYS PAT CHILDREN
ON THE HEAD WHENEVER
YOU MEET THEM,
JUST IN CASE THEY
HAPPEN TO BE YOURS.

Augustus John

IN DOG YEARS, I'M DEAD.

Anonymous

TRUE TERROR IS TO
WAKE UP ONE MORNING
AND DISCOVER THAT
YOUR HIGH SCHOOL
CLASS IS RUNNING
THE COUNTRY.

Kurt Vonnegut

RED MEAT
AND GIN.

Julia Child on the
key to her longevity

MIDDLE AGE IS HAVING
A CHOICE BETWEEN
TWO TEMPTATIONS
AND CHOOSING THE
ONE THAT'LL GET
YOU HOME EARLIER.

Dan Bennett

WHEN GRACE IS JOINED
WITH WRINKLES, IT IS
ADORABLE. THERE IS
AN UNSPEAKABLE DAWN
IN HAPPY OLD AGE.

Victor Hugo

ONE MAN IN HIS TIME PLAYS MANY PARTS.

William Shakespeare

I'M NOT INTERESTED
IN AGE. PEOPLE WHO
TELL ME THEIR AGE
ARE SILLY. YOU'RE AS
OLD AS YOU FEEL.

Elizabeth Arden

MIDDLE AGE IS
WHEN YOUR OLD
CLASSMATES ARE SO
GREY AND WRINKLED
AND BALD THEY DON'T
RECOGNISE YOU.

Bennett Cerf

ALL WOULD LIVE LONG, BUT NONE WOULD BE OLD.

Benjamin Franklin

GROWING OLD IS LIKE
BEING INCREASINGLY
PENALISED FOR A
CRIME YOU HAVEN'T
COMMITTED.

Anthony Powell

THERE WILL ALWAYS
BE DEATH AND TAXES;
HOWEVER, DEATH
DOESN'T GET WORSE
EVERY YEAR.

Anonymous

I REFUSE TO ADMIT THAT
I AM MORE THAN 52,
EVEN IF THAT MAKES MY
CHILDREN ILLEGITIMATE.

Nancy Astor

PUSHING 40?
SHE'S HANGING ON
FOR DEAR LIFE.

Ivy Compton-Burnett

REGRETS ARE THE
NATURAL PROPERTY
OF GREY HAIRS.

Charles Dickens

I DON'T HAVE
ANY CHILDREN,
I HAVE FOUR
MIDDLE-AGED
PEOPLE.

Dick Van Dyke

THE YEARS BETWEEN
50 AND 70 ARE
THE HARDEST. YOU
ARE ALWAYS ASKED
TO DO THINGS, AND
YET YOU ARE NOT
DECREPIT ENOUGH TO
TURN THEM DOWN.

T. S. Eliot

THE PAST IS THE ONLY DEAD THING THAT SMELLS SWEET.

Cyril Connolly

AN ARCHAEOLOGIST IS
THE BEST HUSBAND
A WOMAN CAN HAVE:
THE OLDER SHE GETS,
THE MORE INTERESTED
HE IS IN HER.

Agatha Christie

MEMORIAL SERVICES ARE THE COCKTAIL PARTIES OF THE GERIATRIC SET.

Harold Macmillan

YOUTH IS THE TIME OF
GETTING, MIDDLE AGE
OF IMPROVING, AND OLD
AGE OF SPENDING.

Anne Bradstreet

THE YOUNG SOW
WILD OATS, THE
OLD GROW SAGE.

Winston Churchill

YOU DON'T GET OLDER, YOU GET BETTER.

Shirley Bassey

THE LONG DULL
MONOTONOUS YEARS
OF MIDDLE-AGED
PROSPERITY OR MIDDLE-
AGED ADVERSITY
ARE EXCELLENT
CAMPAIGNING WEATHER
FOR THE DEVIL.

C. S. Lewis

MRS ALLONBY: I DELIGHT IN MEN OVER 70, THEY ALWAYS OFFER ONE THE DEVOTION OF A LIFETIME.

Oscar Wilde

MY IDEA OF HELL IS TO BE YOUNG AGAIN.

Marge Piercy

ANYONE CAN
GET OLD. ALL
YOU HAVE TO DO
IS LIVE LONG
ENOUGH.

Groucho Marx

I DO WISH I COULD
TELL YOU MY AGE
BUT IT'S IMPOSSIBLE.
IT KEEPS CHANGING
ALL THE TIME.

Greer Garson

HE WAS EITHER A
MAN OF 150 WHO WAS
RATHER YOUNG FOR
HIS YEARS, OR A MAN
OF 110 WHO HAD BEEN
AGED BY TROUBLE.

P. G. Wodehouse

I HAVE WRESTLED WITH
DEATH. IT IS THE MOST
UNEXCITING CONTEST
YOU CAN IMAGINE.

Joseph Conrad

A MAN LOVES THE
MEAT IN HIS YOUTH
THAT HE CANNOT
ENDURE IN HIS AGE.

William Shakespeare

YOU KNOW YOU'RE
GETTING OLD WHEN
THE CANDLES COST
MORE THAN THE CAKE.

Bob Hope

THE YOUNG HAVE
ASPIRATIONS THAT
NEVER COME TO
PASS, THE OLD HAVE
REMINISCENCES OF
WHAT NEVER HAPPENED.

Saki

TO ME, OLD AGE IS
ALWAYS 15 YEARS
OLDER THAN I AM.

Bernard Baruch

TO STOP AGEING
KEEP ON RAGING.

Michael Forbes

YOU'RE ONLY YOUNG
ONCE, BUT YOU CAN
ALWAYS BE IMMATURE.

Dave Barry

IF YOU RESOLVE TO GIVE
UP SMOKING, DRINKING
AND LOVING, YOU DON'T
ACTUALLY LIVE LONGER.
IT JUST SEEMS LONGER.

Clement Freud

THE FIRST SIGN OF
MATURITY IS THE
DISCOVERY THAT THE
VOLUME KNOB ALSO
TURNS TO THE LEFT.

Jerry M. Wright

YOU'RE NEVER TOO OLD TO BECOME YOUNGER.

Mae West

AGE SELDOM ARRIVES
SMOOTHLY OR QUICKLY.
IT'S MORE OFTEN A
SUCCESSION OF JERKS.

Jean Rhys

OLD AGE ISN'T SO BAD
WHEN YOU CONSIDER
THE ALTERNATIVE.

Maurice Chevalier

FOR THE BEST GRANDPARENT IN THE WORLD

FOR THE BEST GRANDPARENT
IN THE WORLD

Hardback

£5.99

978-1-84953-674-5

*Grandparents are there to help the child get
into mischief they haven't thought of yet.*

Gene Perret

Grandparents are a constant source of understanding,
advice and love. This beautiful collection of quotations
will make every grandparent see how much they are
appreciated and loved.

IT'S
ALWAYS
WINE
O'CLOCK

IT'S ALWAYS WINE O'CLOCK

Hardback

£5.99

978-1-84953-534-2

Wine is the most civilised thing in the world.

Ernest Hemingway

A swift half, a cheeky tipple, a tall glass of something special – the world of drink is full of delights, fit for any occasion. Celebrate the joy of aqua vitae with this collection of wit and wisdom from the most quotable quaffers!

@EsmeTheBird

If you're interested in finding out more about our books, find us on Facebook at **Summersdale Publishers** and follow us on Twitter at **@Summersdale**.

www.summersdale.com